The best 100 | Spanish recipes

P&M
EDICIONES

Introduction

Spanish cuisine could be described as a rich blend of the various specialties from the country's different regions, a reflection of their traditions and customs.

Anyone visiting the Basque Country, for example, should not fail to order a portion of *marmitako*, a typical fisherman's dish from the region, invented by the cooks on board who prepared this savoury recipe using the scarce resources which they had to hand. Similarly, a visitor to Barcelona should try a dish of traditional Catalan broad beans or grilled vegetables, while Castile offers "Tripe, Madrid Style" and Valencia has its famous paella. Throughout the country, the traditional Spanish omelette or *tortilla* is a dish guaranteed to please visitors and one which never fails. Sauces and relishes, such as the *mojos* from the Canary Islands, also form part of this rich intermarriage of cultures and recipes. Without them, many dishes would lose much of their quality, as well as depriving diners of the opportunity to indulge in the quintessentially Spanish custom of "mopping-up".

This book is a compendium of tastes and flavours aimed at the reader who wishes to know more about a country that offers a rich variety of culinary products — meat, game, fish, sauces, soups, eggs, pulses and vegetables — and ways of preparing them. Combined together they represent a unique and unmistakable expression of Spanish culture and identity.

soups

Ajo blanco con uvas

White garlic soup

- 250 gr breadcrumbs
- 150 gr raw crushed almonds
- 1 unsprouted garlic clove
- 1 egg
- 2 tbsp vinegar

- 1 glass olive oil, 0.4° acidity
- 1/2 l water

GARNISH:
- 100 gr grapes
- 50 gr currants and salt

preparation

Soak the bread for an hour then strain it. • Pulverise all the ingredients in a food blender for 5 minutes then strain them through a fine sieve. • Cool the mixture in the fridge. If it is too thick, add ice or more water.

Presentation: Add grapes and currants as a garnish on the top of the soup.

Caldo gallego
Galician soup

- 3 l water
- 100 gr white haricot beans
- 2 medium potatoes
- 1 onion
- 200 gr offcuts of *Serrano* ham
- 1 ham knucklebone
- 1 handful turnip greens
- 2 tbsps pork lard
- Salt to taste

preparation

Leave the beans to soak. • The next day, put them in a large pan, with the ham offcuts, the knucklebone, the onion and the lard. Cover with 3 litres of cold water and leave it to cook until the beans are almost tender. Then add the potatoes, the greens and salt. • Continue cooking until it is ready. • Adjust the seasoning and serve very hot.
Presentation: Garnish with the *Serrano* ham offcuts cut into strips.
Note: If it is necessary to add water during cooking, make sure it is hot so the soup does not go off the boil.

Crema de calabaza
Pumpkin soup

- 1 1/2 kg pumpkin
- 3/4 kg potatoes
- 1 onion, chopped
- 2 cloves of garlic, chopped
- 1 dl olive oil

- 1 meat stock cube
- Salt
- 1 dl water
- 1 small cup of cream

preparation

Fry the onion; once it is sautéd add the garlic, the potatoes and the pumpkin. • After a few minutes, add a meat stock cube to the water and let it boil until the potatoes are tender. • Blend it in the blender until it has the consistency of a smooth cream and add the cream, warming it through for a few more minutes.

Presentation: Can be garnished with chopped parsley or chopped spring onion stalks.

Gazpacho

Gazpacho (cold tomato soup)

- 250 gr bread
- 1 kg ripe tomatoes
- 1 strip green pepper
- 1 clove garlic
- 50 gr cucumber
- 1 dl oil
- 1 tbsp vinegar
- Salt and a pinch of sugar

- Water

GARNISH:
- 1/2 cucumber
- 1/2 green pepper
- 1 tinned red pepper
- 1/2 onion
- 1 hard boiled egg
- Cubes of fried bread

preparation

Soak the crumbled bread for a few hours. • Introduce the previously squeezed-out bread into the cup of the food processor with the tomatoes, pepper, cucumber, garlic, oil, salt, sugar and a small glass of water. • Process for a few minutes to create a smooth emulsion. • Pass through a sieve and tip into a bowl. If too thick, dilute with more water.

Presentation: Serve with ice cubes. The vegetables and egg should be chopped up fine separately. Serve the garnish around the soup or on a separate tray.

Purrusalda

Leek soup

- 3/4 kg potatoes
- 12 leeks
- 1/4 kg crumbled salt cod
- 1 onion, chopped
- 1 bay leaf
- 1 dl olive oil
- 1 meat stock cube
- Salt

preparation

Peel the potatoes and cut them up. Get rid of the green part of the leeks and take off the outer layer of the white part. Cut into 3 centimetres pieces. Leave the salt cod to soak for 12 hours, changing the water 2 or 3 times.

The broth: Lightly sauté the onion and leek in oil. When they are transparent add the potatoes and salt. Cover with water and add the bay leaf and the meat stock cube. When the leeks and potatoes are cooked add the fish. When the water begins to boil, test the broth. Season with water and salt and serve.

Salmorejo

Salmorejo (gazpacho cream)

- **1 kg ripe tomatoes**
- **1 clove of garlic**
- **1 full cup of breadcrumbs**
- **1/4 l olive oil**
- **1 tsp vinegar (optional)**
- **1 pinch of sugar**
- **Salt**
- **100 gr Jabugo ham in strips**
- **2 hard-boiled eggs**

preparation

Introduce the tomatoes and the garlic into the cup of the food processor. • Having processed them, add the bread and process a little more. • With the mixer working, add the oil little by little. • When the oil is used up, season and process again on the highest setting to make an emulsion. Put in the fridge.

Presentation: Serve very cold in individual bowls accompanied by strips of ham and hard-boiled egg.

Sopas de ajo

Garlic soup

- **1 dl oil**
- **1 head of garlic**
- **1 onion**
- **1 tomato**

- **1 tsp mild paprika**
- **Eggs**
- **Bread**

preparation

Fry the garlic cloves in the oil and set aside. In the same oil sauté the onion and chopped tomato. • Once well sautéd, add the teaspoon of mild paprika and cover with abundant water. • Add the garlic cloves, previously crushed, season the broth and allow it to cook. • At the last moment add the eggs and poach for three minutes. When the soup is ready, toast some slices of bread and place on top.

Sopa castellana

Castilian soup

SOUP:
- 2 l water
- 1 meat stock cube
- 1 onion
- 1 carrot
- 1 stick of celery
- 200 gr *Serrano* ham
- 100 gr fresh *chorizo* sausage
- 2 hard-boiled eggs, chopped
- 150 gr sliced bread
- Salt to taste

TOPPING:
- 1/4 dl oil
- 2 unsprouted garlic cloves, chopped

preparation

Start to cook all the elements of the soup listed above. • After half an hour, take out the ham and the *chorizo* and chop. • Continue to cook for a further 20 minutes.

The topping: Sauté the garlic cloves and re-fry the mixture of *chorizo* and ham.

To assemble: Add the bread, the fried mixture and the hard-boiled egg to the soup. Taste and adjust the seasoning. It is ready for serving when it starts to boil again.

rice and pasta dishes

Arroz a banda

Arroz a banda (rice platter)

- 1 kg fish offcuts
- 3 whole peeled onions
- 2 whole peeled potatoes
- 1 head of garlic
- 400 gr rice
- Oil

- Salt
- 1 tsp paprika
- 2 bay leaves
- 2 tbsp tomato sauce
- Saffron and parsley
- *Alioli* sauce (page 122)

preparation

The broth: Heat water in a large pan, meanwhile sauté in a frying pan in abundant oil the potatoes, onions, garlic cloves and bay leaves. When they start to brown, add the paprika and tip into the pan with the boiling water. After 30 minutes add the fish, leaving until it is cooked. Once done, drain the broth in order to separate the fish, the onions and the potatoes. Set them aside. • **The rice:** Put the paella pan on the flame having added the oil and tomato sauce. Sauté the paprika in the pan and add the rice. Next add the boiling broth (double the amount of liquid to that of rice) and put it in the oven at 250 degrees for 20 minutes. Having removed it from the oven, place a lid over the rice and leave it for 10 minutes.
Presentation: Serve with *alioli* sauce.

Arroz al horno
Rice in the oven

- 125 gr chickpeas
- Half a small cabbage
- 400 gr rice
- 2 medium potatoes
- 3 tomatoes
- 1 red pepper

- 1 head of garlic
- 1 rice *morcilla*
- 1 dl oil
- Saffron
- Salt

---

preparation

Soak the chickpeas for 12 hours, then cook them with the cabbage until tender. When just cooked, season with salt and a pinch of saffron. Drain and set aside on a plate. • In a frying pan fry separately the pepper cut into strips, the potatoes, the tomatoes and the *morcilla* cut into slices. In the same oil sauté the rice and the chickpeas. Then tip them into an earthenware casserole dish. • In the centre of the dish place the head of garlic and around it the potatoes, the *morcilla*, the tomato and the strips of pepper alternating with each other. Adjust the salt and saffron. • Heat up the broth (double amount of liquid to rice) and when it starts to boil, pour it over the rice and put the dish into the oven at 250 degrees for 20 minutes.

Arroz caldoso con almejas y pescado
Rice in broth with clams and fish

- 2 1/2 l fish stock
- 3 cloves of garlic, chopped
- 1 cup of rice
- 1 green pepper, chopped
- 1 onion, chopped
- 1 cup of tomato sauce

- 1 tomato, peeled and diced
- 250 gr clams
- 1/2 kg hake ear
- 1/2 kg squid
- 1 1/2 dl oil

preparation

Clean and chop the vegetables. • Cut each hake ear in half and clean. • Empty the squid, turning them inside out, clean and cut into rings. • In a pressure cooker cook the vegetables until they are well poached, add the rice and salt. Add the half ear and the squid. • Pour the fish stock on top and the cup of tomato sauce, season with salt, pepper and aromatic herbs. • Close the pressure cooker and time for 7 minutes until the valve rises and take off the heat. • In a frying pan sauté the clams until they open. • Having taken the lid off the pressure cooker, add the clams and serve immediately.

Arroz negro

Black rice with squid ink

- **200 gr rice**
- **1/2 kg squid**
- **1 dl olive oil**
- **1 sweet dried red pepper**
- **Parsley**

- **1 head of garlic**
- **3 ripe, peeled tomatoes**
- **1 lemon**
- **Salt**
- *Alioli* **sauce (page 122)**

preparation

Clean the squid, cut into rings and cook, without taking out the sack of ink, with double the amount of water to rice. • Put the paella pan on the heat with the oil. Once heated up, fry the dried pepper, take out and put into a mortar with the garlic, oil, parsley, lemon and ripe tomatoes to make a paste known as *salmorreta*. • Tip the paste into the same oil, the squid ink and the rice and sauté for a while. • Add the squid with its broth, season with salt and cook for 20 minutes.
Presentation: Leave to rest for 5 more minutes and serve with *alioli* sauce.

Canalones
Cannelloni

- 12 cannelloni
- 200 gr tomato sauce (page 123)
- 50 gr grated cheese

FILLING:
- 1 onion, finely chopped
- 1 clove of garlic, chopped
- 50 gr thick tomato sauce (page 123)

- 1 250 gr tin of tuna fish or 1/2 kg of minced meat, sausage or *cocido* leftovers
- Salt and pepper

BECHAMEL SAUCE (page 122):
- 30 gr flour
- 30 gr butter
- 1/4 l milk

preparation

Cook the pasta "al dente" in boiling, salted water with a splash of oil.

The filling: Sauté the onion, garlic and tomato in a frying pan with a little oil. Cook for a few more minutes until the onion is soft and add the tuna fish (or whatever other ingredient chosen). Season.

How to assemble: Lay the cooked pasta out on the table. Put a teaspoon of filling on one side and roll up, laying the closed side down so that the cannelloni do not open. • Cover the bottom of an oven dish with tomato sauce, place the filled cannelloni on top and layer with the bechamel sauce. Sprinkle with grated cheese and cook au gratin in the oven.

Fideuá

Fideuá (noodle paella)

- **250 gr thick noodles**
- **2 green peppers**
- **4 garlic cloves**
- **1/2 kg squid**
- **1/2 kg prawns**

- **1 dl olive oil**
- **3/4 l fish stock**
- **Salt**
- ***Alioli* sauce (page 122)**

preparation

Heat the oven to 250 degrees. In a frying pan, fry the prawns for a few minutes and peel. Boil the heads of the prawns and pass them through a puré sieve. Reserve the stock. • Sauté the garlic, the peppers and the squid in the paella pan. Next, add the noodles and stir until they are well sautéd. • Pour onto this the boiling stock from the prawns, topping up with water if necessary. Place in the oven for 20 minutes. • At the end, add the prawns.
Presentation: Serve with *alioli* sauce.

Paella

- 2 large cups of rice
- 300 gr prawns
- 100 gr pork loin, diced
- 10 chicken wings
- 1 1/2 dl olive oil
- 3 garlic cloves

- 1 tomato, peeled and diced
- A few drops of lemon juice
- Salt and saffron
- 4 cups of stock from the prawns
- 2 hard-boiled eggs and one tinned red pepper

preparation

Peel the prawns, fry the tails for a few seconds and set aside in the fridge. • Cook the heads in water for 30 minutes, pass through the puré sieve. • Leave the hot stock to one side on the heat. • Season the meat with salt and pepper. • In a paella dish sauté the garlic, chicken and pork in oil. • Add the rice, stirring for 5 minutes. • Add the lemon, tomato, salt, pepper and crushed saffron. • Pour the hot prawn stock over, add additional hot water if necessary. • When it starts to boil, cook in the oven at 180 degrees for 20 minutes then leave to stand for another 15 minutes out of the oven. • If the rice is too hard and dry, sprinkle some water over it by hand, put the lid on and cook for a few more minutes.

Presentation: Decorate with fried prawn tails, the hard-boiled eggs and the pepper.

vegetables

Cardos con salsa de almendras
Cardoons with almond sauce

• 1 kg cardoons	SAUCE:
BROTH:	• 3 cloves of garlic, chopped
• 1 tbsp flour	• 1/2 small glass of olive oil
• 1 tbsp olive oil	• 1/4 l stock from the cardoons
• 1 lemon	• 50 gr ground almonds
• 3 l water	• 1 tbsp flour
	• Salt and pepper

preparation

Dissolve the flour in 3 litres of water and add a few drops of lemon juice and oil. • Remove the fibres from the cardoon stalks, cut into 4 centimetres pieces, rub with lemon to avoid discoloration and cook in a pressure cooker for 20 minutes.

The sauce: Sauté the garlic and add the almond, the flour and the stock from the cardoons. Season with salt and pepper.

To complete: Once the sauce is ready, add the cardoons, leave to cook for a few more minutes and serve.

Espinacas con pasas y piñones
Spinach with currants and pine nuts

- **500 gr frozen spinach**
- **100 gr pine nuts**
- **100 gr currants**
- **100 gr butter**

- **2 cloves of garlic, finely chopped**
- **2 tbsp olive oil**
- **Salt and ground pepper**

preparation

Soak the currants for 4 hours. • De-frost the spinach leaves and chop them very finely. • In a frying pan, with the butter and oil, sauté the pine nuts and the garlic until brown, add the currants which have been lightly dusted in flour, followed by the spinach. Sauté for 6 minutes until the liquid given out from the spinach leaves evaporates.

Habas a la catalana
Catalan broad beans

- 1 kg broad beans
- 200 gr white Catalan sausage (butifarra blanca)
- 2 rashers of bacon, chopped
- 2 cloves of garlic, chopped
- 1 onion, chopped
- 1 small glass of *Oloroso* sherry
- 1 small glass of olive oil
- 8 sprigs of mint, chopped
- Salt

preparation

Shell the broad beans. Take the outer skin off as well, if possible. Set aside. • In an earthenware casserole, sauté the onion and garlic, add the bacon and when all the ingredients are transparent, add the broad beans. • Cover the mixture with water. • Add the sherry, the chopped mint, salt and water to cover. • Cook until the broad beans are tender. • Add the sausage in slices.

Presentation: Serve garnished with the rest of the mint.

Judías verdes con jamón
Green beans with *Serrano* ham

- 2 kg flat green beans
- 1 onion, chopped
- 2 tomatoes, peeled and chopped
- 3 cloves of garlic, chopped
- 100 gr acorn-fed *Serrano* ham in strips
- Oil and salt

preparation

The sauté: sauté in oil the onion, garlic and tomato, adding the ham last. Season.

The beans: Normally good quality beans do not need the string removing, but do so if necessary. Alternatively, cut them down lengthways to make them finer. Cook them "al dente" in boiling salted water and when ready pass them under the cold tap so that they retain their colour. Add them to the sauté mixture and leave to cook for a few minutes.

Lechugas braseadas
Braised lettuce

- 6 Tudela baby lettuce hearts
- SAUCE:
- 3 onions, chopped
- 3 shallots, chopped
- 2 tbsp toasted flour
- 1 dl olive oil

- 3/4 meat stock
- Salt and pepper
- THE BATTER:
- 2 eggs
- Flour
- Abundant olive oil

preparation

Cook the lettuce hearts in boiling salted water for 8 minutes. Cut them down the middle and drain. Dip in flour and egg and fry, then set them aside on a heat-proof dish.

The sauce: Sauté the onions in oil. When transparent, add the shallots and sauté for a further 15 minutes. Sprinkle with the toasted flour and add the hot stock. Cook for 10 minutes and season. Pass the mixture through a fine puré sieve and pour over the lettuce hearts.

To complete: Cover with tin foil and cook in the oven for one hour at 160 degrees.

Menestra navarra

Navarran vegetables

- 500 gr artichokes
- 500 gr carrots, diced
- 500 gr peas
- 500 gr green beans
- 700 gr mushrooms, sliced
- 1/2 dl olive oil
- 1 onion, finely chopped

- 2 leeks, finely chopped
- 2 rashers of bacon cut into julienne strips
- Salt

GARNISH:
- 2 hard-boiled eggs
- Triangles of fried bread

preparation

Wash all the vegetables, cut the ends off the beans, peel the carrots and pod the peas, take the stalks off the mushrooms. Cut down the tall leaves of the artichokes around the heart by about a third and sprinkle with lemon juice. • Make a stock with the vegetable remmants. First cook the carrots and the peas then add the mushrooms and green beans 10 minutes later. When they are ready strain the vegetables and retain the stock. • Slowly fry the onions and leeks in oil in a deep frying pan. • Add a glass of the vegetable water, season and add the bacon and the rest of the vegetables. Sauté for a few more minutes. • **Presentation:** Place the vegetables on a dish decorated with the hard-boiled egg and triangles of fried bread.

Papas arrugás con mojo picón
Wrinkled new potatoes with *mojo picón*

- **2 kg new Canarian potatoes**
- **Water**
- **Sea salt**
- ***Mojo picón*** (page 125)

preparation

Choose potatoes of the same size, so that they cook equally. • Once thoroughly washed, put them into a large saucepan, cover with water and add a few large pinches of coarse sea salt. • When the potatoes are tender tip away any remaining water and allow them to dry so that they wrinkle and the salt sticks to them.

Mojo picón: Grind up the garlic and peppers in a mortar. When well crushed, add pepper, and the oil and vinegar slowly. Make a thick or light sauce to taste. Serve as an accompaniment to the potatoes.

Patatas con costillas

Potatoes with ribs

- 1 kg potatoes, chopped
- 1/2 kg pork ribs
- 1 onion, finely chopped
- 1 green pepper, finely chopped

- 1 red pepper, chopped
- 1 clove of garlic, chopped
- 1 dl oil
- Water and salt

preparation

Fry the onion in a cooking pot. • When it starts to go golden, add the peppers, the garlic and the chopped ribs. Sauté for a few minutes. • Next add the potatoes, coating them. Cover the whole with water, and leave to cook on a low heat until tender. • Season and serve very hot.

Patatas en camisa (importancia)

Dressed potatoes

- 1 kg potatoes
- 2 eggs, beaten
- Flour
- Abundant oil
- TOPPING AND SAUCE:
- 1 dl oil

- 3 cloves of garlic, chopped
- 2 tbsp *Oloroso* sherry
- 7 threads of saffron
- Salt
- 1 tbsp flour
- 1 l water

preparation

Peel and cut the potatoes into fine slices. • Dip in egg and flour. • Fry one by one in abundant oil and drain.

The topping and sauce: Sauté the garlic in the oil. Before it goes brown add the saffron and flour pounded together. Stir and add the sherry and the water. Cook the fried potatoes in this mixture. Season with salt. When ready adjust the thickness of the sauce. If too runny, add a spoonful of flour dissolved in tepid water. • Bring to the boil and serve.

Patatas en salsa verde con pescado
Potatoes in green sauce with fish

- 1 kg potatoes, cut into pieces
- 2 onions, chopped
- 2 cloves of garlic, chopped
- 3 tbsp parsley, chopped
- 1 dl oil
- 1/2 kg frozen fish in pieces without skin or bones
- Water and salt

preparation

Sauté the onion in the oil for five minutes and then add the garlic and the potatoes. • Let them absorb the oil well, then cover with water and season. • When the potatoes are tender, add the parsley and fish, letting it all cook a little longer until ready. • Serve very hot.

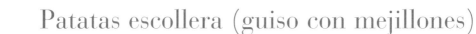

Patatas escollera (guiso con mejillones)
Breakwater potatoes (mussel stew)

- 1 kg potatoes
- 1 onion, chopped
- 1 leek, chopped
- 2 green peppers
- 1 garlic

- 1 tomato
- 1 kg mussels
- Parsley
- Salt

preparation

In a casserole, sauté the onion, the pepper, the leek, the tomato and a little salt in oil. • When the mixture is almost ready, add the chopped potatoes, sauté well and cover with water, allowing them to cook for around 30 minutes. • Sauté the garlic until golden, add the cleaned mussels, cover with a lid and wait until they open. Take them out of their shells and add them to the potatoes with the strained stock.

To complete: Heat through for a few more minutes and serve with chopped parsley on top.

Pimientos rellenos de arroz
Rice-filled red peppers

- **8 red peppers**
- **400 gr rice**
- **100 gr *chorizo*, chopped**
- **100 gr bacon**
- **150 gr pork loin**

- **500 gr ripe tomatoes**
- **1 clove of garlic, chopped**
- **Parsley**
- **Oil**
- **Salt**

---

preparation

Wash the peppers, take out the stalks and lids by cutting around them with a knife and set them aside. • Empty the peppers, carefully removing the seeds and the main interior veins. • Cook the rice in boiling water for 10 minutes. • Sauté the chopped garlic with the *chorizo*, the bacon, the pork loin, half the tomato and the rice. • Once everything is sautéd, fill the peppers with the mixture, closing them with the stalks and lids previously cut out. Hold them together with a cocktail stick.

To complete: Place the lightly oiled peppers in an oven dish, and pour the rest of the tomato on top of them. • Put them in a previously heated oven for 45 minutes at 180 degrees.

Pimientos del piquillo rellenos de bacalao
Red *piquillo* peppers stuffed with cod

- 200 gr salted cod in small pieces
- 1 tin of red *piquillo* peppers (about 425 gr), of which 2 peppers should be set aside for the sauce
- Bechamel sauce (page 122)
- A few drops of concentrated meat stock
- Salt

preparation

Soak the salt cod for 48 hours. Keep it in the fridge and change the water about 6 times. When it is ready to cook, put it in cold water and heat up, removing it just before the water boils. Clean the skin and spines and break it up small. • Prepare a white sauce and divide it into two parts. • To one part, add the cod and quickly bring to the boil and remove. Fill the peppers with this mixture and place them in an oven dish.

The pepper sauce: To the other half of the white sauce add the peppers and the meat stock. Blend them in a food mixer and pour over the peppers in the dish. Cook in the oven for half an hour at 180 degrees.

Pisto

- **500 gr of courgettes, peeled and diced**
- **300 gr green peppers, chopped**
- **150 gr tomatoes, poached and peeled**
- **100 gr onion, chopped**
- **1 red pepper**
- **Olive oil**
- **Salt, pepper and sugar**
GARNISH:
- **2 hard-boiled eggs**

preparation

Roast the red pepper for 1 hour wrapped in tin foil. • Let it cool down covered, then peel and dice it. • Sauté the onion in 2 decilitres of oil. After 5 minutes, add the green peppers, and after 15 minutes add the courgettes and the red pepper. Season and let it stew slowly. • After half an hour add the tomatoes, and cook everything together slowly for 10 more minutes. • Finally, let it rest and skim off any surface fat. • If it is too liquid, let it cook a little longer and season.
Presentation: Decorate with the hard-boiled eggs.

30

Rovellones o níscalos
Milk cap mushrooms

- **1 kg milk cap mushrooms**
- **100 gr bacon**
- **3 garlic cloves, chopped**
- **1 onion, finely chopped**
- **1 dl olive oil**
- **Salt**

preparation

Clean the mushrooms without wetting them, then rinse them several times until they are free of mud. • Finely slice the heads and rinse them again. • Sauté the onion in the oil. • Once it is transparent add the garlic, the bacon cut into julienne strips and the mushrooms, which should be cooked until the liquid they exude has evaporated.

Tumbet

- 3 aubergines
- 8 fresh red peppers
- 6 medium potatoes

- 1 l tomato sauce (page 123)
- Olive oil
- Salt

preparation

Cook the red peppers at 200 degrees wrapped in tin foil for 45 minutes. Wait until they cool down, then peel them and cut them into strips. • Peel the potatoes and cut them into fine slices. Dip them in flour and fry. • Cut the aubergines into slices and arrange the ingredients in an oven dish in the following order: first the potatoes, then the aubergines, then the peppers. Cover the whole with the tomato sauce. • Bake in the oven for one hour at 170 degrees and serve.

salads

Cogollitos de Tudela

Tudela baby lettuce hearts

- **6 small lettuce hearts**
- **2 strips of chopped smoked ham or bacon**

THE DRESSING:
- **1 tsp sherry vinegar**
- **4 tbsp extra virgin olive oil**
- **Salt and pepper**

preparation

Take off the outer leaves of the lettuces and clean them well, passing them under the cold tap. Cut them in half lengthways. • Fry the bacon. Prepare the dressing, beating together the ingredients, then add the bacon.

To complete: Pour the dressing over the lettuce hearts.

Ensalada de naranja y bacalao
Orange and cod salad

• 2 oranges	THE DRESSING:
• 500 gr cod	• 1 small glass of olive oil
• 1 onion	• 3 tsp white wine vinegar
	• 1 garlic clove
	• Salt, pepper and a pinch of sugar

preparation

Cut the orange into segments and take off the pith. • Break up the fish and soak in water while preparing the other ingredients. Chop the onion into very fine julienne strips.
The dressing: Crush the garlic clove and mix with the vinegar, whisk with the oil and season.
To complete: Place on a dish the orange segments, onion and the drained cod on top. Pour the dressing over it and serve.

Ensalada de pato
Duck salad

- 2 tomatoes, peeled and cut into small cubes
- 1 Tudela baby lettuce heart, chopped
- 150 gr green beans, cut into fine strips and cooked "al dente"
- 2 avocados cut into strips

- 150 gr bacon
- 150 gr duck ham

THE DRESSING:
- 3 tbsp olive oil
- 1 tbsp Balsamic vinegar
- 1 tsp sugar
- Salt

preparation

Sauté the tomatoes and place them in the centre of a serving plate. • Next place the finely chopped lettuce, the sautéd green beans and the avocado, and lastly the duck ham on top of the avocado slices. Fry the bacon until very crispy. • Sprinkle the bacon over the salad.
To complete: Make a dressing with 3 tablespoonfuls of oil for one of vinegar, salt and a pinch of sugar. • Combine the dressing ingredients thoroughly and pour over the salad.

Ensalada tibia de langostinos
Warm king prawn salad

- Salad leaves
- 6 artichoke hearts
- 2 garlic cloves, chopped
- 200 gr button mushrooms
- 24 king prawns

THE DRESSING:
- 1/2 dl stock from the prawns
- The prawn shells
- 3 tbsp oil
- 1 tbsp vinegar
- 2 shallots
- Salt and pepper

preparation

Wash and dry the salad leaves. Finely slice the artichoke hearts and the mushrooms and sauté in a small amount of oil. Peel the prawns and sauté them with the garlic.
The dressing: Sauté the heads and shells of the prawns in a little oil, crush them so that they give off all their juice, add a little water and let the mixture reduce on the heat. • Strain and mix with the oil. Chop the shallots and mix with the oil of the prawns and the vinegar. • Season and beat over the heat with a whisk.
Presentation: Arrange the salad leaves first on a plate, next the artichokes, the mushrooms and the prawns. Pour over the dressing.

Ensalada de gambas

Prawn salad

- 1 kg prawns
- 1/4 home-made mayonnaise (page 123)
- 1 tbsp condensed milk
- 2 apples, peeled and cut into pieces

- 1 lemon
- 1 lettuce, chopped

THE DRESSING:
- 1 tbsp Balsamic vinegar
- 3 tbsp extra virgin olive oil
- Salt and pepper

preparation

Mix the mayonnaise with the condensed milk. Peel and sauté the prawns and add them to the above. • Peel the apples, cut them, sprinkle with lemon juice and combine them with the prawn mixture. • Make a dressing for the lettuce.

Presentation: On a plate lay out the lettuce first then the apples and prawns covered with the mayonnaise.

Escalivada

Escalivada (Catalan Style grilled vegetables)

- 2 potatoes
- 2 onions
- 2 green peppers

- 2 aubergines
- Salt
- Virgin olive oil

preparation

Wash the vegetables and the potatoes, cut them into very fine rings and arrange them in order in a large oven dish. • Sprinkle with salt and splash a little olive oil over them by hand. • Cover them with tin foil and roast in the oven for 30 minutes at 170 degrees. When ready, take them out of the oven. • Next, grill them in the oven, laid out on the rack. The vegetables are ready when they start to blacken. Sprinkle them with oil again.

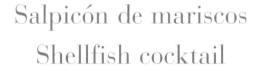

Salpicón de mariscos
Shellfish cocktail

- 1 spring onion cut into strips
- 1 1/2 kg small king prawns, 50 gr each
- 3 large red prawns (*carabineros*)
- 1 kg mussels
- Bay leaves

THE DRESSING:
- 1 dl extra virgin olive oil
- 1 tbsp sherry vinegar
- Salt

preparation

Boil 1 litre of water with 40 grams of salt and two bay leaves. • When boiling fiercely put the prawns and *carabineros* in. The prawns need to cook for 90 seconds and the *carabineros* for 1 or 2 minutes more (depending on size). • Take them out individually when ready and leave them to cool. • Once cold, peel and cut them into slices. • Wash the mussel shells well and put them into a frying pan with a little water to cook. • As they start to open, take the mussels out of their shells.

The dressing: dissolve the salt in the vinegar and beat up with the oil. • Add the spring onions and shellfish. • Ideally, leave for a few hours before serving.

pastry and fillings

Coca de sobrasada
Pork sausage pastry

FILLING:
- 200 gr pork sausage
- 2 tbsp packet onion soup
- 1 tbsp Pedro Ximénez
  sweet wine
- 1 tbsp sugar

PASTRY:
- 1 dl oil
- 1/2 dl white wine
- 2 eggs
- 20 gr fresh yeast
- 1 tbsp salt and 1/2 tbsp sugar
- 300 gr flour

preparation

The pastry: Dilute the yeast in tepid white wine. Add the oil and the beaten eggs. Stir and pour in the flour mixed in with the salt and the sugar. Work for 10 minutes to form a very flexible dough and roll it out to a round shape, pinching the edges with the fingers to lift it up and make the case bigger. Pinch the inside with a fork.

The filling: Leave the sausage-meat to cool down. Add the sweet wine and the onion soup and stir until it makes a smooth paste. • Cover the pastry with the filling. Cover it with tin foil and bake in the oven at 180 degrees for 25 minutes. Half-way through, take off the tin foil and check the cooking so that the top does not burn.

Note: Puff pastry can be used instead.

Croquetas de jamón de Jabugo
Croquettes with *Serrano* ham

- **Bechamel sauce (page 122)**
- **30 gr *Serrano* ham**
- **Salt**
- **Nutmeg**

THE BATTER:
- **2 eggs**
- **Breadcrumbs**
- **Abundant olive oil**

preparation

Make a bechamel sauce with 60 gr of flour and the same amount of the other ingredients. • Add the ham, mixing well. After boiling, let it cool down completely covered with a piece of kitchen paper so that it does not form a crust. • Make the croquettes, giving them shape with a spoon. • Dip them in beaten egg and then in the breadcrumbs. Mould them again. • Fry in the oil at 170 degrees.

Note: The quantities of flour and milk are approximate as the flour absorbs more or less liquid depending on humidity. The essential point is that the bechamel should be thick.

Empanada gallega
Galician filled pastry

FILLING:
- 2 dl olive oil and salt
- 3 onions, chopped
- 4 *piquillo* red peppers, tinned
- 1 tomato, peeled and chopped
- 3 tins of sardines in oil or 1 kg fresh sardines

PASTRY:
- 500 gr flour
- 1 1/2 dl oil
- 1/2 dl cream or milk
- 3 beaten eggs
- 1 tbsp salt and 1 of sugar
- 30 gr fresh yeast

preparation

The filling: Sauté the onions and the peppers in the oil. Scrape off the scales of the fish and take out the backbone. Add them to the onions. When the onions are transparent, add the tomato and salt. Sauté until very well cooked.

The pastry: Dilute the yeast in the luke-warm cream or milk. Add the wine, the oil and 2 beaten eggs. Add the flour, the salt and the sugar. Knead by hand or in a food mixer for 10 minutes until the dough becomes flexible. • Once done, divide it into 2 parts. Roll out one part and fill it with the filling. Place the other rolled out part on top.

To complete: Brush the surface with a beaten egg and bake in the oven for 25 minutes.

Empanadillas de carne
Meat filled pastries

- **Frozen puff pastry, or bought** *empanadilla* **pastry, or home-made pastry (page 124)**
- **200 gr roasted or stewed meat**
- **1 dl tomato sauce (page 123)**
- **A few drops of Worcester Sauce (Lee & Perrins)**
- **A few drops of Tabasco (optional)**
- **1 beaten egg**
- **Salt**

preparation

Chop the meat in a food processor and mix with the tomato sauce and the Worcester Sauce. If required, add a few drops of Tabasco to taste. Season with salt. • Spread out the dough and form into round shapes of 7 centimetres diameter. Divide the filling between them and close them, sealing them with a little beaten egg. Mark the edges with a fork. • Fry in abundant oil. **Note:** The pastry can be made beforehand but the finished *empanadillas* must be fried shortly after filling.

Migas sorianas

Breadcrumbs from Soria

- 1 round durum wheat loaf
- 3 cloves of garlic
- 2 tbsp paprika
- 2 tbsp water
- 3 tbsp oil
- 50 gr *Serrano* ham in small cubes
- 12 slices of *chorizo*

preparation

This recipe is best prepared the night before. • Crumble the bread without the crust. Chop the garlic and mix it with the water and the paprika. • Sprinkle the breadcrumbs with this mixture and stir well so that they absorb the liquid equally. • Make a ball of the mixture and wrap in a damp cloth. • Leave for 12 hours. • Fry the breadcrumbs in a very small amount of olive oil. They should be toasted without becoming saturated with fat. • Crush them and stir, adding the ham and the *chorizo*.

Note: This recipe should be eaten freshly made.

beans and pulses

44

Alubias blancas con almejas
Haricot beans with clams

- **200 gr haricot beans**
- **1/2 kg clams**
- **1 onion**
- **1 clove of garlic**
- **1 bay leaf**

- **White wine**
- **Oil**
- **Parsley**
- **Salt**

preparation

Having soaked and drained the beans, place them in a large cooking pot with the onion, the chopped garlic, bay leaf, parsley and olive oil. • Cover with cold water and leave to cook slowly. • Wash the clams well, put them in an earthenware casserole or frying pan with 2 tablespoons of water and 4 of white wine and leave to boil until they open. • Add the open clams and the strained stock to the beans. • Bring to the boil quickly and serve.

Alubias rojas de Tolosa
Red Tolosa beans

- **400 gr of red beans**
- **1 pig's ear and tail**
- **1 chunk of *Serrano* ham (500 gr)**
- **1 onion**
- **2 whole garlic cloves**
- **3 leeks**
- **Salt**
- **Olive oil**
- **Paprika**

preparation

Soak the beans overnight. • When ready to cook put the beans, onion, garlic cloves, ear, tail and chunk of ham in a large saucepan with cold water and a dash of olive oil. • Half-way through cooking, when everything is almost tender, add a mixture of the onion sautéd with paprika. Leave to cook a little longer until all is thoroughly cooked and season with salt.

Cocido madrileño
Madrid Style cocido

- 200 gr chickpeas
- 1 small cabbage
- 2 carrots and 2 large potatoes
- 2 onions and 3 leeks, whites only
- 1 chunk of *Serrano* ham
- 150 gr pork belly
- 1 piece of cured pork shoulder

- 1/4 chicken
- 1 1/2 kg beef *morcilla* (blood sausage)
- 2 *chorizos* (250 gr) and 1 rice *morcilla*
- 1/2 l tomato sauce
- 2 tbsp oil
- 2 garlic cloves, chopped
- 150 gr noodles

preparation

Leave the chickpeas to soak for 12 hours the night before. • In a large cooking pot put the pork shoulder, the smoked bacon, the beef *morcilla*, the chicken and the chickpeas to cook in water. • When the chickpeas are almost tender, add the vegetables. • Take the various ingredients out as they are ready (about 4 hours). • Cook the cabbage separately. Once ready, drain and sauté in a little oil with the chopped garlic on a slow heat. Add the *chorizo* and the *morcilla* and keep cooking for another 20 minutes. • **To complete:** Cook the noodles in the stock, while preparing the various serving dishes. On one place the chickpeas, vegetables and meats and on the other the cabbage, the chopped smoked bacon and the hams and sausages. All can be accompanied by the tomato sauce.

Fabada asturiana

Asturian white bean casserole

- 1/2 kg dried lima beans
- 2 pork *morcillas* (blood sausages)
- 2 small *chorizos*
- 1/4 kg cured pork
- 100 gr streaky salt pork
- A few strands of saffron
- A dash of oil
- Salt

preparation

The night before, soak the cured pork in tepid water and the beans in cold water. • In a pan cook the beans, the cured pork, the *morcillas*, the *chorizos*, the streaky salt pork and a dash of oil: everything should be covered with the same cold water that the beans were soaked in the night before. • Having started to boil, reduce the heat and leave to cook slowly, making sure that the beans are always covered in water so that they do not lose their skins. • Half-way through cooking add the lightly-toasted saffron, broken down very fine. • Once cooked, season the beans and break up a few spoonfuls of them by passing them through a hand puré to add thickness to the stew. • Continue to cook very slowly for a few more minutes.

Gachas

Gachas (pork casserole)

- **4 tbsp oil**
- **4 tbsp vetch flour**
- **2 pork steaks**
- **Bacon**
- **100 gr pork belly**

- **2 cloves garlic, chopped**
- **200 gr *chorizo***
- **2 tsp mild paprika**
- **1/2 tsp hot paprika**

preparation

Fry the meat and the chopped smoked ham. Once fried, set them aside. • In the same oil, add the garlic cloves, the *chorizo* and the chopped bacon. When cooked, set them aside. • In the remaining oil sauté the flour and the paprika, stirring constantly so that they do not stick. When well cooked, add 4 ladles of stock or water and leave to boil for 15 minutes.

Presentation: Serve in an earthenware casserole dish garnished with the bacon, ham and *chorizo*.

Garbanzos con espinacas y bacalao
Chickpeas with spinach and salt cod

- 300 gr chickpeas
- 1 whole, peeled onion
- 2 whole, unpeeled cloves of garlic
- 2 cloves of garlic, chopped

- 200 gr frozen spinach
- 150 gr crumbled salt cod
- 1 dl olive oil
- Salt

preparation

The cod: Soak in water for 24 hours, changing the water various times. • Leave to soak in salt water overnight.

The chickpeas: Soak in salt water overnight. Pour away this liquid, add them and cook in 4 times as much water, adding the onion and the garlic cloves. • When almost done, take out the onion and the garlic and pass them through the puré sieve. • Cover the bottom of a frying pan with oil and sauté the 2 chopped garlic cloves, adding the puré of onion and garlic and the spinach and cod. Tip this over the chickpeas. Season with salt and continue cooking until the chickpeas are ready.

Note: It is difficult to specify cooking times, given the difference between types of chickpeas.

Lentejas con chorizo
Lentils with *chorizo*

- 400 gr lentils
- 1 onion, finely chopped
- 1 onion, whole
- 1 garlic clove
- 1 carrot cut into pieces
- 100 gr pork belly
- 1 tsp mild paprika
- 150 gr *chorizo*

preparation

Soak the lentils for a few hours. Cook in cold water with the pork belly, the whole onion, the carrots and the paprika. • Half-way through cooking, fry separately the chopped onion and the garlic. Add the cooked onion and the carrots from the casserole. • Once sautéed, pass the whole through a puré sieve and add to the lentils. • When almost cooked, add the *chorizo* and allow to cook for a few minutes.

Presentation: Serve the *chorizo* cut into slices and the pork belly chopped in pieces.

eggs

51

Huevos abuñuelados fritos con arroz y pimientos
Puffed-up fried eggs with rice and peppers

- **6 eggs (50 gr each)**
- **1 cup of white rice**
- **6 red peppers**

- **2 garlic cloves, chopped**
- **Olive oil**

preparation

Fry the eggs one by one in abundant oil at 190 degrees. • As they start to fry, re-shape the edges with the slotted spoon and cover the yolks with the whites, so that turn into puffed-up balls. • Remove them from the oil and place them on a round plate. • Roast the peppers covered in tin foil in the oven at 180 degrees for an hour. • Let them cool down, covered, and then peel them and cut them into strips. • In a frying pan, sauté the garlic, the peppers and their juice. • Once the rice is cooked, put it into a bowl, turn it out onto the middle of the dish and arrange around alternately with the eggs and the strips of pepper.

Huevos al nido

Eggs in a nest

- **6 brioches**
- **6 eggs**
- **4 slices of cooked ham**
- **100 gr grated cheese**

- **12 tbsp white sauce (page 122)**
- **Salt**
- **Pepper**

preparation

Cut a lid off the brioches and empty the middle. • At the bottom of each one put 2 tablespoons of white sauce, the chopped ham, the cheese and an egg yolk. Season. • Beat the egg whites until they form peaks and cover the brioches with them one by one. • Bake until the whites are golden. They can also be fried in abundant oil.

Presentation: Can be served with tomato sauce.

Huevos encapotados
Muffled-up eggs

- 6 eggs
- Bechamel sauce (page 122)

BATTER:
- 2 eggs
- Breadcrumbs
- Abundant oil for frying

preparation

Fry the eggs in abundant, very hot oil. • Then place them one by one and separated on a platter. • Next, prepare the bechamel and when ready pour over the eggs and leave to cool. • Coat with egg and breadcrumbs and fry.

Presentation: Accompany with straw potatoes and tomato sauce.

Huevos estrellados

Broken eggs

- **1 1/2 kg potatoes**
- **2 garlic cloves, peeled**
- **6 medium eggs**
- **Salt**
- **Abundant olive oil**

preparation

Peel the potatoes and cut them length-wise, 3/4 centimetres thick. • When the oil reaches a temperature of 175 degrees, add the potatoes in batches and fry. • Control the heat so that the potatoes cook inside without turning golden. When ready, strain them through a colander. • Leaving a layer of oil in the pan, put the potatoes back in it. • While the potatoes heat up again, break the eggs over them one by one, deliberately breaking them. Season.

Revuelto de ajetes

Scrambled eggs with garlic shoots

- 100 gr tender garlic shoots
- 4 eggs
- 2 tbsp cream

- Salt
- 3 tbsp oil

preparation

Cut the garlic shoots halfway down the stalk and chop into small strips of 3 centimetres, only using the white part. • Sauté in a frying pan with oil until they are soft. Once ready, season. • Beat the eggs, add a pinch of salt and mix them with the cream. • Pour the mixture into the frying pan with the garlic shoots. • Stir until the eggs set and the mixture becomes creamy.

Revueltos con langostinos y espinacas
Scrambled eggs with king prawns and spinach

- 8 eggs
- 8 king prawns
- 300 gr frozen spinach
- 2 tbsp cream

- Oil
- Salt

preparation

In a frying pan, sauté the well-chopped spinach in 3 tablespoons of olive oil. • Cook and peel the prawns and sauté them with butter. Set aside. • Break the eggs into a bowl, adding cream and salt. • Cook in a bain-marie for 8 minutes, moving them continually with a whisk. • When they are cooked, add the prawns and the spinach.
Presentation: Serve with triangles of fried bread.

Tortilla de calabacín
Courgette omelette

- 6 eggs
- 2 dl oil
- 1 kg unpeeled courgettes
- 2 onions, chopped
- Salt

preparation

In 1 decilitre of oil fry the onion slowly, seasoned with salt. • Wash the courgettes and without peeling them, cut them into fine slices and fry with the onion until transparent. Don't fry them too much or they will fall apart and loose flavour. Take off the heat and place in a strainer to get rid of all the moisture. • Once well drained, heat them in a non-stick frying pan with 1 decilitre of oil. • Beat the eggs in a bowl, season and pour over the courgettes, mixing carefully. Lower the heat so that it sets slowly. • Using the lid, flip over the omelette and cook the other side until it sets.

Tortilla de patatas
Tortilla (Spanish potato omelette)

- 1 kg potatoes
- 200 gr onion, chopped
- 8 eggs (50 gr each)

- 1 dl olive oil, 0.4° acidity
- Salt

preparation

Peel the potatoes and cut them into thin slices. • Heat the oil in a 25 centimetres diameter non-stick frying pan and add the potatoes. • After 5 minutes add the onion and salt. Keep the heat high, and move the potatoes with a spatula every now and then so that they do not stick, lifting them off the bottom. When they are soft strain them in a colander. • Mix the potatoes with the beaten eggs, stirring them once. Add more salt to taste. • Heat 3 tablespoons of the poured off oil in a frying pan and when it starts to smoke, add the egg and potato mixture. Move the frying pan so that the tortilla does not stick and shape the edges with a slotted spoon to round them off. Lower the heat and let the tortilla cook slowly. • When it is still slightly runny inside, tip it over onto a plate and slide it back into the frying pan so that the other side cooks for a few seconds and goes brown.

Tortilla de pimientos del piquillo y bacalao
Omelette with red *piquillo* peppers and cod

- 100 gr onion, chopped
- 400 gr green peppers, seeded and chopped
- 3 cloves of garlic
- 8 tinned red *piquillo* peppers

- 100 gr cod in small pieces
- 8 eggs
- 5 1/2 tbsp oil
- Salt

preparation

Soak the cod for 12 hours, changing the water 3 times. • In a 20 cm frying pan sauté the onion in oil. • When transparent, add the garlic and the green peppers and cook until tender. Add the red peppers and the cod and sauté all together with 1/2 tbsp of oil. The mixture should be cooked for 5 minutes without letting the cod start to go brown. Season. • Beat the eggs and add them to the mixture. • Let the omelette cook on a very slow heat. • When set but still slightly runny inside tip it over onto a plate and slide it back into the pan so that the other side sets and turns brown.

meat and poultry

Albóndigas de ternera
Beef meat balls

- 500 gr young beef, chopped
- 3 sausages
- 40 gr smoky bacon
- 4 slices of sliced white bread
- 1 dl dl cream
- 2 eggs
- 1 clove of garlic, finely chopped
- 1 tbsp parsley

- Flour and salt

THE SAUCE:
- 1 onion, chopped
- 1 carrot, finely chopped
- 1/2 tomato, peeled and chopped
- 1 tbsp toasted flour
- 2 dl oil
- 1 meat stock cube and salt

preparation

Ask the butcher to mince up the smoky bacon with the meat. Add the sausage meat, removed from its skin. Soak the bread in the cream and mix it in a food mixer with the eggs, salt, chopped garlic and parsley. Once mixed, pour the mixture over the meat. Knead it all together, make balls and dip them in flour. • Fry in very hot oil to form a crust.

The sauce: Heat the onion and when it is transparent, add the carrot, the tomato and the salt. Add the toasted flour, 2 glasses of water and a meat stock cube. Cook for 30 minutes then pass through a puré sieve. Heat the meat balls in the sauce for 15 to 20 minutes.

Caldereta de cordero

Lamb stew

- 1 kg lamb, cut into pieces
- 2 onions, finely chopped
- 2 green peppers, chopped
- 1 dl olive oil
- 12 small new potatoes, peeled
- 4 garlic cloves
- 3 bay leaves
- 2 tbsp fresh parsley, chopped
- 1 tbsp paprika
- 1 tbsp sea salt
- Freshly ground black pepper
- 1 tbsp red wine vinegar
- 1 heaped tbsp flour

preparation

Sauté the onions and the peppers in the oil. Lightly salt the pieces of lamb and add them to the onions. Sauté for a few seconds. • Grind the garlic, bay leaves, parsley, paprika, salt and pepper together and dissolve it all with the vinegar and a little water. Pour over the meat and onions and totally cover with water. • After half an hour, add the potatoes and allow to cook until ready. • Add the flour dissolved in a little of the water to bind the sauce and allow it to come to the boil.

Presentation: Divide into 6 earthenware bowls, and serve very hot.

Carrilleras

Jawbones

- **1 kg jawbones**
- THE STOCK:
- **2 onions**
- **2 carrots**
- **2 cloves of garlic**
- **1 tbsp brandy**
- **1 meat stock cube**
- **Salt**
- **Pepper**
- **1 tbsp corn flour**
- BATTER:
- **Flour**
- **Egg**
- **Olive oil for frying**

preparation

Remove the greasy parts from the jawbones and place them in cold water for 6 hours to drain the blood. • Put them in a pressure cooker with all the ingredients for the broth and cook for 20 minutes from the moment the valve rises. • Once cooked and cooled down, cut into fillets, dip in egg and flour and fry. Place on kitchen paper to absorb excess fat. • Reduce the broth and pass it through a puré sieve. • Bind the sauce with a tablespoon of corn flour dissolved in water and add the jawbones. Cook for a short time and serve.

Chuletón de buey con pimientos del piquillo
Beef chop with red *piquillo* peppers

- **4 beef chops (500 gr each)**
- **12 red *piquillo* peppers**
- **2 garlic cloves**
- **1 tbsp oil**
- **Coarse salt**

preparation

Heat the barbecue with wood-burning fuel or wood (must be hard-woods) which should burn up without making too much smoke. It is important to wait until the grill is really hot and only the embers are left. • At this point, put on the chops, sprinkled with salt. Take them off when the meat is red inside and toasted on the outside.

To complete: Fry the garlic cloves in hot oil with the peppers (de-seeded) and sauté slowly, stirring frequently.

Presentation: Place the chop on a very hot plate, garnished with the peppers.

Cochinillo asado
Roast suckling pig

- **1 suckling pig,
  maximum 1 month old**
- **1 glass of dry white wine**
- **Oil or pork lard**
- **2 garlic cloves**

- **1 onion**
- **6 black peppercorns**
- **1 small glass of vinegar**
- **Bay leaves and salt**

preparation

Salt the piglet, previously cleaned and cut down the middle. Marinade it for several hours with the wine, garlic, chopped onion, peppercorns, bay leaves and salt. • Rub it with the pork fat and put it in a pre-heated oven at 170 degrees. • Half-way through cooking turn it over and brush with vinegar. This should be done 4 or 5 times every 10 minutes to ensure that the skin comes out crispy. • Cooking time will be around an hour and a half.

Note: Suckling pig is usually accompanied by a garnish of roast potatoes and a lettuce salad.

Estofado de morcillo de ternera con verduras
Calves' foot stew with vegetables

- 1 kg calves' foot
- 2 dl olive oil
- 2 onions, finely chopped
- 2 carrots
- 250 gr peas
- 150 gr turnip

- 2 dl white wine
- 2 1/2 dl cream
- 2 egg yolks
- 1 lemon
- 1 clove, salt and pepper

preparation

Season the meat with salt, pepper and crushed clove. • Fry until golden in olive oil. • Cut up turnips and the carrots. • In the pan with the meat add the onions and the rest of the vegetables and fry for a few minutes. • Pour the wine over it, adding some water, and allow to cook until the meat is tender. • Break the eggs, adding a few drops of lemon, mix with the cream and heat without boiling for a few minutes.

To complete: Cut the meat into slices and accompany with the sauce and vegetables.

Gallina en pepitoria
Chicken in almond sauce

- 1 2 kg chicken
- 3 onions, chopped
- Flour for frying
- Olive oil

- 1 l chicken stock
- 4 threads saffron
- 50 gr ground almonds
- Parsley and salt

preparation

Chop the chicken into pieces, season, dip in flour and fry. • Sauté the onions and place them in a casserole with the chicken. • Sprinkle the chicken with parsley and the pounded saffron and cover with the stock. • Cook slowly for an hour. • At the end add the almond and leave to boil for a few more minutes.

Presentation: Serve with white rice.

Jabalí en salsa

Boar in sauce

- 1 leg of boar
- 2 coarsely chopped onions
- 2 coarsely chopped tomatoes
- 2 carrots, diced
- Olive oil
- 3 tbsp aromatic herbs

THE MARINADE:
- 2 carrots, chopped

- 2 onions, in rings
- 6 garlic cloves, chopped
- 4 bay leaves
- Thyme and parsley
- 20 peppercorns
- 1 l red wine
- 2 dl vinegar
- Olive oil

preparation

The marinade: Sauté the vegetables, sprinkle with all the liquids and cook in a pressure cooker for half an hour. • Season the meat with salt and pepper and the aromatic herbs. • Once cold, pour the marinade over the boar's leg and keep for 4 days in a cool place, turning every now and then. • **Roasting the meat:** Roast the meat with abundant oil and place in the oven at 200 degrees for 20 minutes, turning it so that it cooks on all sides.
To complete: Add the vegetables and continue roasting at 150 degrees for another 3 hours.
Note: If the leg has been boned, reduce the roasting time.

Lacón con grelos

Cured pork shoulder with greens

- 3 kg cured pork shoulder
- 1 handful greens
- 1/2 kg lightly cured *chorizo*

- 1 kg potatoes
- 1 dl olive oil

preparation

Wash the pork shoulder in tepid water to remove the salt from the surface and leave submerged in water for 2 hours. • Put the meat in a pan with abundant water and the oil and when it starts to boil add the *chorizo* and the greens. • Boil for another hour and add the potatoes. • After half an hour, strain off all the liquid and serve the meat very hot.
Presentation: Serve all the ingredients on a dish. Another option is to serve the pork and *chorizo* cut into pieces and the greens and potatoes separately.

Pechugas de pollo en escabeche
Chicken breasts in marinade

- 2 kg chicken breast

THE MARINADE:
- 1/4 l olive oil
- 1/4 l white wine
- 2 dl vinegar
- 2 dl water

- 1 chopped onion
- 4 garlic cloves, mashed
- 10 peppercorns
- 1 meat stock cube
- Bay leaves
- Salt

preparation

Put the marinade in a casserole dish and heat until boiling. Add the chicken breasts and cook with the lid on for 20 minutes. • Take out the breasts and put them in a bowl, pouring the marinade over them. • When totally cold, put the lid on and place in the fridge.
Presentation: Serve the chicken breasts in their own gelatine, accompanied by lettuce salad or Russian salad.

Perdices con níscalos y boletus

Partridges with milk cap mushrooms and boletus

- 3 partridges
- 2 dl olive oil
- 1 onion, chopped
- 6 garlic cloves, unpeeled
- 1 bay leaf
- 1/4 l Rioja red wine
- 1 glass water
- 1 tsp mixed herbs
- Salt
- Sauce of milk cap mushrooms and boletus (page 125)

preparation

Clean the partridges. • Pound the garlic and rub over the birds. Season and fry in a casserole with the onion, the garlic and the bay leaf. Pour the wine over and add some water until covered. • Cook for one hour and a half, taking the birds out of the casserole when they tender. • Prepare the sauce of milk cap mushrooms and boletus.

Presentation: Cut the partridges down the middle and cover with the mushroom sauce, very hot.

Perdiz estofada de Toledo
Stewed partridge, Toledo Style

- 2 partridges
- 1 leek
- 1 onion, cut in pieces
- 1 carrot, cut in pieces
- 1 l fried tomato puré (tinned)
- 4 shallots

- 1 small glass brandy
- 1/2 kg button mushrooms
- 50 gr smoked bacon
- Olive oil
- 1 lemon
- Salt

preparation

Clean the partridges and rub with lemon. • Add 3 or 5 spoonfuls of oil to a casserole dish and fry the birds on all sides. • Add the onion, the carrot, the leek, the shallots and the bacon. Sauté thoroughly. • Pour the brandy over and flambé. • Add the tomato and cook until the partridges are tender. Season, adding water if necessary. • Pass through a puré sieve and pour into the casserole along with the mushrooms. • Bring to the boil for a few minutes and serve.

Pierna de cordero rellena
Stuffed leg of lamb

- 1 boned leg of lamb
THE MARINADE:
- 4 garlic cloves
- 2 bay leaves and 1 bunch of thyme
- 3 tbsp vinegar
- 2 glasses of olive oil
- Salt and 8 peppercorns
THE STUFFING:
- 75 gr fresh sausages

- 1 lamb's liver
- 1 slice of sliced white bread
- 3 tbsp cream
- 1 egg, chopped thyme and salt
THE MEAT GLAZE:
- 1 glass of white wine and 1 of marinade
- Corn flour
THE GARNISH:
- Fried aubergines in batter

preparation

The marinade: Mix the ingredients and cover the leg. Leave to marinade for 2 hours. • **The filling:** Chop the liver and mix with the rest of the ingredients of the filling. Place all into the cavity left by the bone and press down well. Seal the edges with tin foil. • **The meat glaze:** Season the leg and brown it on both sides. Pour the wine and the marinade over it. When it begins to boil, put the lid on and cook in the oven for 40 minutes at 200 degrees. • Dip the aubergines in flour and egg and fry in olive oil. • **Presentation:** Cut the leg into slices and present on an oval dish in its own juice with the aubergines.

Pollo al ajillo
Chicken with garlic

- 1 chicken, cut into pieces
- 3 garlic cloves, chopped
- 6 garlic cloves, unpeeled
- 1/2 dl *fino* sherry
- 2 dl olive oil
- Salt

preparation

Rub the chicken pieces with the chopped garlic and salt. • Put the oil in an earthenware casserole and when warm add the chicken and unpeeled garlic cloves, letting them fry until golden. • Add the wine and allow to boil until it has reduced.

Pollo al chilindrón

Chicken with sweet peppers

- 1 chicken, cut into pieces
- 1 chunk of *Serrano* ham
- 4 red peppers
- 4 tomatoes, peeled

- 1 onion, chopped
- 3 cloves of garlic, chopped
- Flour, olive oil and salt

preparation

Roast the red peppers covered in tin foil for 45 minutes. • Leave to cool in the oven so that they sweat, then peel them, removing the seeds. Cut them into small cubes. • Dip the pieces of chicken in flour and fry. Take out and set aside. • In a casserole dish sauté the onion and when transparent add the garlic and ham. • Next, add the tomato and the peppers and after 15 minutes the pieces of chicken, leaving it all to cook for 30 minutes.

Rabo de toro

Oxtail

- 2 bulls' tails, cut into pieces
- 4 onions, chopped
- 2 carrots, cut into pieces
- 6 garlic cloves, crushed
- 2 dl olive oil
- 2 tbsp brandy
- 3 twists of milled black pepper
- Red wine
- Salt

preparation

Place the tails in a casserole so that they fit snugly. • Heat the onions in the oil and when transparent, add the garlic and the carrots. Season and tip over the meat. • Add the brandy and enough wine to comfortably cover. Put a lid on the casserole, heat it on the top and when boiling, put it in the oven at 100 degrees. • After 4 hours check to see if the tails are tender, take them out and place them on a dish. • Skim the fat off the liquid and pour it over the tails. Serve very hot.

Note: Can be done in a pressure cooker but it can overcook, so needs very careful supervision.

Ropa vieja
"Old clothes" (Hash)

- **1 kg cooked blood pudding (*morcilla*)**
- **1/2 l tomato sauce (page 123)**
- **2 red peppers**
- **2 garlic cloves**
- **1/2 chilli pepper**
- **Salt, paprika, pepper and sugar**

preparation

Make the tomato sauce beforehand. • Roast the peppers wrapped in tin foil for 60 minutes at 180 degrees. Once cold, peel them, cut them into strips and place in an earthenware dish with the chopped garlic and tomato sauce. • Season with salt, a little paprika, pepper and sugar. • Cut the *morcilla* (already cooked) and add it to the sauce. Cook in the oven for 3 minutes at 160 degrees.

Note: This is a useful recipe for using up leftovers of roast meat.

Solomillo de corzo

Venison steaks

- 3 venison steaks
- 2 onions, chopped
- 1 small glass of olive oil
- 3 tbsp brandy

THE MARINADE:
- 2 onions, cut into julienne strips
- 3 garlic cloves, chopped
- 4 bay leaves
- Thyme and rosemary

- 20 black peppercorns
- 1 glass of white wine
- 3 tbsp raspberry vinegar

SAUCE:
- 2 tbsp honey
- 1/2 l stock from the meat juices (see below)
- 1 tbsp raspberry vinegar
- 1 tsp corn flour

preparation

The marinade: Mix all the ingredients cold and marinade the steaks for 12 hours.

The glaze: Season the steaks and fry them lightly until golden. Set aside. • In the same fat sauté the onions and when transparent put the meat back in, sprinkle with brandy and a glass of the marinade and allow to cook for 15 minutes on a slow heat.

The sauce: Dissolve the honey with the vinegar, add the meat juices and the onion from the glaze. Bind with a teaspoon of corn flour.

fish

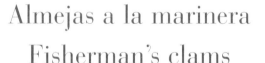

Almejas a la marinera
Fisherman's clams

- 1 kg clams
- 4 cloves of garlic, chopped
- 1 dl olive oil
- 1 dl white wine
- 2 dl broth from the clams

- 2 tbsp parsley, chopped
- 1 tbsp flour
- Salt
- Water

preparation

Knock the clams against each other to remove the fine sand and soak in salt water. After half an hour wash and cook in 2 decilitres of water. Take them out as they open. • Strain the stock and set it aside. • Heat the garlic in the oil and, before it changes colour, add a tablespoon of flour dissolved in the wine and the stock from the clams. • When it boils, add the clams and sprinkle over the parsley. Only requires 1 or 2 minutes' cooking time.

Angulas vascas al pil-pil
Basque elvers sizzled in garlic

- 1 1/2 kg baby eels
- 3/4 l olive oil, 0.4° acidity
- 12 cloves of garlic
- 8 small pieces of dried chilli pepper
- Salt

preparation

Divide the elvers into 8 earthenware dishes. • Place a piece of red pepper on top of each. • Sauté the garlic in oil. • Strain this oil and pour it boiling over each dish, constantly stirring the elvers so that they heat up equally. Must be served very hot.

Bacalao al pil-pil
Cod sizzled with garlic

- 12 thinly-sliced pieces of cod
- 1 tbsp parsley, chopped
- 2 dl olive oil

- 6 garlic cloves, sliced
- A few drops of chilli oil
- Water

preparation

Soak the cod to de-salt it for 24 hours, changing the water various times. • Fry the garlic in an earthenware casserole, removing before it changes colour. • Let the oil in the casserole cool completely, then introduce the pieces of cod with the skin upwards. • Move the casserole from side to side so that the sauce starts to bind, turning the fish over. • Add a tablespoon of water and another of oil, and continue to move the dish, without letting it boil as this would break down the sauce.

Completing the dish and presentation: Gradually add more water and oil depending on how the sauce thickens. It should become a sort of light bechamel. When done, sprinkle with parsley. **Note:** This recipe takes 15 minutes from the moment of starting to move the casserole dish around.

Bacalao a la vizcaína
Biscay salt cod

- **1 kg boneless, thick fillet of cod**
- **4 onions, chopped**
- **4 leek stalks, white parts only, chopped**
- **10 dried sweet red peppers ("choricero" type)**
- **4 garlic cloves, peeled**
- **2 slices of baguette bread, fried**
- **1 dl oil for the sauté**
- **1 dl oil to complete the dish**
- **1 tbsp breadcrumbs and salt**

preparation

Soak the cod, divided into pieces, for 48 hours in 3 litres of water, changing the water several times. Ideally, keep it in the fridge. • Soak the peppers for 12 hours then scrape out the flesh, setting it aside for the sauce. • **The sauce:** Cover the bottom of a pressure cooker with oil and sauté the vegetables in the following order: onions, leeks, garlic, the flesh from the peppers and a little salt. • Add the fried bread and cover with water. • Close the pan and time it for 30 minutes from the moment the valve rises. • Once cooked, pass through a puré sieve and tip into an earthenware casserole. • Cook the de-salted cod in abundant cold water, taking it out just before it boils, strain and place on top of the hot sauce. • **To complete:** Fry the breadcrumbs rapidly in clean oil and sprinkle over the stew. Cover with tin foil and bake in the oven at 170 degrees for a few minutes until the cod has heated through. If cooked for too long it will spoil.

Besugo a la espalda
Bream with garlic and chilli peppers

- 1 1 1/2 kg bream
- 1 dl olive oil
- 2 garlic cloves, chopped
- Vinegar

- 1 dl oil
- 3 pieces of chilli pepper
- Salt

preparation

Ask the fishmonger to de-bone the fish. • Place it in an oven dish with the skin down. Season and pour over the olive oil, cooking in the oven for around 17 minutes at 170 degrees. • Fry the garlic and chilli until golden.

To complete: Once the fish has been taken out of the oven, sprinkle the garlic and chilli mixture over it and a few drops of vinegar. • Serve hot.

Bonito donostiarra

Tuna, San Sebastian Style

- **2 tuna steaks**
  (250 gr each approx.)
- **2 dl olive oil**
- **2 green peppers cut into rings**
- **A few drops of chilli oil**

- **2 onion, chopped**
- **3 cloves of garlic**
- **5 ripe tomatoes**
- **Sugar**
- **Salt**

preparation

Cut the tomatoes with a cross shape through the stalk and put them into boiling water for 5 minutes. • Sauté the ingredients in the following order: onion, then after 5 minutes the garlic and peppers, and after 15 minutes the peeled and chopped tomatoes. • Season with chilli oil, salt and sugar and cook for one hour. • Place the fish in an oven dish and pour over the hot sauce. • Cook in the oven for 15 minutes at 180 degrees.

Bonito encebollado
Tuna with onions

- 4 tuna steaks (200 gr each)
- 4 dl olive oil
- 1 dl white wine
- 1 tbsp vinegar
- 8 large onions, finely cut into rings
- Salt

preparation

Fry the onion rings very slowly in 2 decilitres of oil. • Season when they are done then add the white wine and cook until reduced, at which point add the vinegar. • Fry the tuna separately in the rest of the oil, leaving it almost raw. Take off the skin and remove the bones, season and add the onions, letting it all cook for another 3 minutes.

Calamares encebollados de Santander
Squid with onions, Santander Style

FOR TWO PEOPLE:
- 6 small squid
- 3 spring onions, chopped
- 1 onion, cut into strips
- 1 leek (white part only) cut into fine strips
- Oil
- Salt

preparation

Clean the squid, taking out the innards and the cartilage that runs down the inside of the body. Wash and set aside the tentacles. • In a frying pan cook the squid on both sides in very hot oil, season. Fry the tentacles separately. • Remove any liquid that they give out from the pan. • Sauté the spring onions, the onions and the leek in a small amount of oil and season with salt. • Divide between two plates and put the squid on top.

Note: With recently caught squid, wait 24 hours before cooking as otherwise they will be very tough.

Caldereta de langosta

Lobster stew

- 2 kg lobster
- 2 dl olive oil
- 3 garlic cloves, finely chopped
- 2 onions, finely chopped
- 1 tbsp concentrated tomato puré
- 50 gr ground almonds

- 2 hard boiled egg yolks
- Salt

THE STOCK:
- 1/2 dl dry white wine
- 1/2 kg small prawns
- 2 onions

preparation

The stock: Chop the onions and sauté slowly with the prawns. Add the white wine and allow to evaporate, then 1 litre of water. Leave to cook until it reduces. Pass it through a puré sieve and set aside. • **The lobster:** Cook (page 128) and cut up, removing the sac from the head. Pour the juice into a mortar and dilute with 2 or 3 tablespoons of water and a pinch of salt. Strip the meat out of the shell and claws and dice. • In an earthenware casserole slowly sauté the onions and garlic in oil. Add the tomato to give colour, the stock from the seafood and the juice from the mortar. Add the hard-boiled egg yolk and the ground almonds. Cook for a few minutes more. • **To complete:** Add the lobster at the last moment and allow to cook for 2 or 3 minutes so that it is juicy. **Presentation:** Accompany with pieces of toast and alioli sauce.

Cocochas de bacalao

Cod cheeks

- **1 kg cod cheeks**
- **4 tbsp olive oil**
- **6 tbsp water**
- **6 unsprouted garlic cloves**
- **A few drops of chilli oil or Tabasco sauce**
- **4 tbsp parsley, chopped**
- **Salt**

preparation

Put the oil, the chopped garlic and a pinch of salt into a large frying pan. • Sauté slowly, without letting the ingredients change colour and leave to cool completely. • Add the cheeks and season with a little more salt. • Heat them up, moving the frying pan backwards and forwards, gradually add 6 tablespoons of water as the sauce thickens. The more water added, the thinner the sauce will be. (It is difficult to specify exactly the amount required). • Add the drops of chilli oil and the parsley. Once the cheeks are well cooked take them off the heat.
Presentation: Divide into 6 small earthenware dishes, with the juice.
Note: Do not boil the sauce while cooking the cheeks.

Chipirones en su tinta

Squid in their own ink

- 24 squid
- 1 onion, chopped
- 2 garlic cloves, chopped
- 1 green pepper, chopped
- Olive oil
- 2 dl tomato sauce (page 123)
- Ink from the squid or 3 sachets of ink
- Salt

preparation

Clean the squid well, taking off the very fine skin that covers them. • Cut off the fins and take out the guts and the bony cartilage that runs inside the body. • Put the tentacles aside and the wide sac that contains the ink. • Wash the outside and turn them inside out like a glove, washing again. • Chop up 6 whole squid and the tentacles and fins of the rest. • Sauté all of this and once done stuff the remaining 18 squid with the mixture.

The sauce: Sauté in olive oil the onion, garlic and pepper. When cooked, add the tomato sauce. Mash up the ink sacs with a little coarse sea salt and add a little water. • Cook the squid in this sauce until tender. • Adjust the salt to taste.

Dorada a la sal

Gilthead bream with salt

- **1 gilthead bream of 3 kg**
- **2 kg of coarse salt**

THE GARNISH:
- *Patatas a lo pobre*
- **Mayonnaise**

preparation

On an oven tray spread a fine layer of salt, then the fish on top and cover with the remainder of the salt. • Splash with a few drops of water and put in the oven for 35 minutes.
Presentation: Accompany with potato casserole *Patatas a lo pobre* and mayonnaise.

Gambas al ajillo
Prawns with garlic

- 300 gr whole prawns
- 1 dl olive

- 5 cloves of garlic, chopped
- 4 small pieces of chilli pepper
- Salt

preparation

Peel the prawns raw and set aside. • In an earthenware casserole tip the oil, the chopped garlic and the chilli pepper. • Heat up without allowing the garlic to go brown. When ready, add the prawns and season in moderation, moving around until they change colour. • Serve very hot.
Note: These quantities are for one portion.

Lubina al horno

Sea bass in the oven

- **4 thick fillets of sea bass (200 gr each)**
- **1 dl olive oil**
- **2 tbsp brandy**
- **1 tbsp butter**
- **2 shallots**
- **3 dl cream**
- **2 tbsp pepper**
- **Salt**

preparation

Put the butter and oil in an earthenware casserole. • Sauté the very finely chopped shallots and before they change colour add the pieces of fish with the skin facing upwards. Brown them for a minute and turn them over. • Flambé with the brandy and add the cream and pepper. Next place in a pre-heated oven at 180 degrees for 6 minutes approximately.

Marmitako

Marmitako (tuna and potato stew)

- 2 dl olive oil
- 2 onions, chopped
- 3 green peppers, cut into rings
- 4 red peppers (piquillo type), tinned, cut into small pieces
- 4 garlic cloves, chopped

- 2 kg potatoes
- 1 kg tuna fish
- 1 1/2 dl fried tomato sauce (page 123)
- Salt
- Pepper
- 1 bay leaf

preparation

Fry the onions in the oil. • Season with salt and add the garlic and green pepper. When almost done, add the red peppers. • When this is ready, add the potatoes cut into medium-sized pieces. • Cover with water and add the fried tomato and the bay leaf, and leave to cook until tender. • Adjust the salt. • Add the tuna in chunks, letting it cook slowly for around 15 minutes.
Presentation: Serve in 6 earthenware dishes.

Merluza en salsa verde
Hake in green sauce

- 4 hake steaks (200 gr each)
- 4 cloves of garlic, finely chopped
- 1 onion, finely chopped
- 3/4 kg clams
- 1/2 small glass of white wine
- Fish stock
- 1 dl olive oil
- Parsley
- Salt

THE GARNISH:
- 12 tips of tinned asparagus
- 3 hard-boiled eggs
- 250 gr tinned peas

preparation

In an earthenware casserole dish put 1 decilitre olive oil and slowly fry the onion and garlic. • Add the pieces of hake. • While cooking, move the dish in a circular movement so that the sauce thickens and add the white wine, the clams, the peas and abundant parsley.
Presentation: Once finished, decorate with the hard-boiled eggs and asparagus.

Rape alangostado
Monkfish lobster Style

- 2 kg thick monkfish fillet
- 1 l fish stock
- 1/4 l dry white wine
- 12 black peppercorns

- Salt
COATING:
- 2 dl olive oil
- 2 tbsp mild paprika

preparation

The monkfish: buy the thickest part of the fillet and ask for it to be de-boned.
Cooking: Tie the fillets separately with twine. • Coat in the paprika and cook in a fish stock prepared earlier with the wine. • Cook for 10 to 12 minutes so that it bubbles slowly.
Presentation: Serve cut into roundels on a bed of salad.

Trucha estofada con jamón
Stewed trout with *Serrano* ham

- **1 1/2 kg trout**
- **100 gr *Serrano* ham**
- **4 cloves of garlic, chopped**

- **2 dl olive oil**
- **Salt**

preparation

Ask the fishmonger to take out the spine of the fish and leave it open. • Place the fish laid out flat in a baking dish with the skin upwards. • Sauté the garlic and pour it in its oil over the trout, covering this with the ham. • Cover with tin foil and bake in the oven for 30 minutes at 180 degrees.

Presentation: Present the trout open, sprinkled with the garlic and oil and covered with fine strips of ham.

Ventresca de bonito
Tuna fillet

- **1 fillet of the tuna stomach**
- **3 garlic cloves**
- **Parsley**
- **Breadcrumbs**
- **Olive oil**
- **Salt**

preparation

Place the cleaned fish in an oven dish. • Chop the garlic cloves and sprinkle over the fish. Next add the olive oil, the parsley, a tbsp of breadcrumbs and salt. Bake for 10 minutes at 170 degrees.

Note: The cooking time depends on the size of the piece of fish. 1 kilo should be cooked for 7 minutes in the oven. • Overcooked fish looses its juicy texture and becomes flaky and tasteless.

tripe and other delicacies

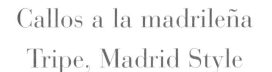

Callos a la madrileña
Tripe, Madrid Style

- 1 1/2 kg tripe
- 1/2 kg chopped snouts
- 1 beef hoof, de-boned and cut into pieces
- 200 gr *Serrano* ham
- 8 dried red peppers
- 100 gr soft (lightly cured) sausage
- 1 *morcilla* (optional)

- Salt and black peppercorns
- 1 dl olive oil
- 2 onions, chopped
- 4 cloves of garlic, chopped
- 1 cup of tomato sauce (page 123)
- 2 cups of the tripe stock
- 1 piece of chilli pepper or a few drops of Tabasco sauce

preparation

Soak the tripe and snouts in water with a good dash of vinegar and some sea salt. After an hour wash in cold water. • Cook in a pressure cooker with water and add the ham, the dried peppers and about 15 black peppercorns. After 45 minutes check the readiness and add the *chorizo*, and the *morcilla* (optional). Cook for another 5 minutes. • To make the sauce, sauté the onion and garlic in oil. When transparent add the tomato sauce, the stock from the tripe and the chilli pepper. • Once done, pass through a puré sieve and pour over the tripe and snouts. • Add the soft sausage and *morcilla*, cut into round slices.

Lengua en escarlata

Tongue in aspic

- 1 veal tongue
- 10 sheets of gelatine (16 gr)

THE STOCK:
- 1 dl olive oil
- 2 leeks and 2 onions
- 2 carrots and 1 turnip

- 1/2 tomato and 1 stick of celery
- 1 dl brandy
- 1 dl Oloroso sherry
- 1 stock cube
- 6 black peppercorns
- A few drops of red vegetable colouring

preparation

Buy the tongue cleaned. Before cooking it has to be rubbed with nitric salt and left in the fridge for 10 hours. Remove, rub with a cloth to remove the salt. • Marinate (page 129) and leave for 6 days in the fridge, removing the liquid that it gives out every day. • On the 7th day, rinse it under the cold tap and leave submerged in water overnight before cooking it in the stock in a pressure cooker. Time it for 30 minutes before the valve rises. When tender, take out and leave to cool down. • Soak the gelatine in cold water and add 1/2 litre of lukewarm water. Heat up without allowing to boil, turning it so that it dissolves well and add the vegetable colouring. Let it cool down and when it starts to thicken paint the tongue about 6 times, waiting for the gelatine to set before painting it again.

Note: This dish cannot be frozen, but it keeps perfectly in the fridge for about 20 days.

Manos de cerdo rellenas
Stuffed pigs trotters

- **6 pigs trotters**
- **THE STUFFING:**
- **300 gr paté de foie-gras**
- **THE STOCK:**
- **1 l white wine**
- **2 onions**
- **2 carrots**
- **Salt and pepper**

- **THE CASE:**
- **Flaky pastry**
- **THE SAUCE:**
- **1 onion, chopped**
- **500 gr button mushrooms**
- **1 tbsp port**
- **1/4 stock cube**
- **1 tsp cornflour**

preparation

Clean the trotters well, burn off any small hairs and wash. • Place in a pressure cooker with all the ingredients of the stock and cook for 25 minutes from the moment the valve rises. • Once tender, allow to cool down and then take out the small bones. • Fill all the openings left by the bones with foie. • Wrap the trotters in very finely rolled flaky pastry and cook in the oven for 10 minutes. • **The sauce:** Fry the onion very slowly; once golden add the port and allow to reduce. Then add the mushrooms and lastly the meat stock, adding a teaspoon of cornflour to thicken if necessary. • **Presentation:** Serve the trotters cold covered with the sauce.

Mollejas en salsa
Sweetbreads in sauce

- 2 kg veal sweetbreads
- 4 onions, chopped
- 4 leeks, chopped
- 8 black peppercorns
- 2 bay leaves
- 4 sprigs of parsley
- *Oloroso* sherry
- Olive oil
- Salt

THE STOCK (2 L):
- 1 kg chicken carcass
- 3 jawbones
- 2 onions
- 1/2 cow hoof
- 1/4 chicken
- 1 leek
- 2 carrots
- 1 tbsp cornflour

preparation

Leave the sweetbreads in cold water for 2 hours. • Next blanch them in boiling water for 3 minutes. • Once cold, clean off the fat. • Prepare the stock. • Sauté the onions and leeks in a little oil then add the sweetbreads and when sautéed, the sherry and stock, leaving them to cook until tender. • Cut into thin slices and cover with the stock, which should be thickened with the cornflour.

sauces and pastry

Salsa alioli
Alioli sauce

- 2 eggs
- 1/4 l olive oil, 0.4° quality
- 2 tbsp water
- 1 tbsp red wine vinegar

- 2 garlic cloves, chopped
- Salt
- 1 pinch of sugar

preparation

Beat the eggs in the blender or with an electric hand blender. • Remove the shoot inside the garlic cloves (if any) and chop. • Add the oil, initially drop by drop, add the garlic and continue beating. As it thickens, the oil can be added in a stream, while continuing to beat until ready. • Lighten the sauce by adding the vinegar and water. Season and beat for a few more minutes.

Salsa besamel
Bechamel sauce

- 70 gr butter
- 40 gr flour
- 1/2 l milk

- Salt
- Pepper

preparation

Melt the better on a low heat and add the flour, cooking slightly. • Add the milk gradually, beating the mixture with a whisk and waiting until it boils before adding more milk. • Once it achieves the correct consistency of cream, season.

Salsa de tomate española
Spanish tomato sauce

- 2 dl olive oil
- 3 onions, chopped (250 gr approx)
- 1 clove of garlic, chopped
- 1 kg ripe tomatoes, chopped

- 1 bay leaf (optional)
- Salt
- Sugar

preparation

Sauté the onion in the oil and season with salt and sugar. • When transparent, add the garlic, the tomatoes and the bay leaf. • While cooking, crush the tomatoes with the slotted spoon. This sauce needs to cook slowly for 2 hours. When done, pass through a sieve or puré.
Note: Should not be processed in a food mixer.

Salsa mayonesa
Mayonnaise

- 2 whole eggs
- 1/2 l olive oil, 0.4° quality
- 1 tsp sherry vinegar
- 2 tbsp water

- Salt
- Pepper
- 1 pinch of sugar

preparation

Put the eggs into the processor/blender and add the oil drop by drop, with the motor running. As it thickens the oil can be added in a stream, continuing to beat until ready. • Then add the water and the vinegar and season. Beat for a few more minutes.
Note: The eggs must be washed well before breaking. In cool weather, this mayonnaise will keep for a week in the fridge, stored in a closed glass jar.

Masa para empanadillas

Pastry for *empanadillas*

- 3 tbsp olive oil
- 3 tbsp milk
- 3 tbsp red wine

- 95 gr approx. flour
- Salt

preparation

Mix the liquid ingredients and season generously. • Add the flour, mixing it manually until it becomes a soft dough. Leave to rest for 1 hour. • Sprinkle the work surface with flour and roll with a rolling pin, spreading out very thin. Make pastry circles of around 7 centimetres. • When ready to use, fill and fry in abundant olive oil.

Note: Pre-made empanadilla cases can be very useful. Also shop-made pastry, which should be rolled out very thin.

Masa quebrada

Short-crust pastry

- 250 gr flour
- 125 gr butter
- 1 egg yolk

- 3 tbsp water
- Salt

preparation

In a large bowl, make a large ring of flour: in the centre place the butter, which should be soft, the egg yolk, the luke-warm water and the salt. • Mix the ingredients together manually and continue to add the flour until it forms a dough. This should be handled as little as possible. Leave to rest for 1 to 12 hours. • After this, sprinkle the work surface with flour and roll the pastry out from the centre to form a circle. • Grease the moulds and cover with the pastry. To prevent it collapsing in the oven, pinch the pastry with a fork and put a small ball of tin foil inside. • Leave again to rest in the fridge for 10 minutes. • Bake for 15 to 25 minutes at 180 degrees. Check the cooking, and when lightly golden remove from the oven.

Note: Frozen manufactured pastry can be used, which saves preparation time, but the result will never be the same as home-made pastry made with natural fats is always much more delicious.

Mojo picón

- 1 garlic clove
- 1 glass of olive oil
- 3 tbsp vinegar
- 3 hot peppers
- 1 tbsp paprika
- Coarse-grained salt

preparation

Make a paste in a mortar with the garlic and peppers. When well mixed, add the paprika and the oil and vinegar slowly. • This sauce can be made thick or thin to taste. It is used as an accompaniment to roast meats and Wrinkled Canary Potatoes (see page 32).

Ragú de níscalos
Milk cap mushroom sauce

- 1 dl olive oil
- 1 kg milk cap mushrooms
- 250 gr boletus
- 2 cloves of garlic, chopped
- 3 onions, chopped
- 30 chopped truffles and their juice
- 1 dl cream
- 2 dl Port
- 1 tbsp tarragon, chopped
- Salt

preparation

Cut the lower stalks off the mushrooms and the boletus, dry and clean the heads with a damp cloth. • Cut them into fine slices and place them on an oven dish. Sprinkle with oil and then with the salt and garlic. • Roast for 20 minutes at 170 degrees. • Cook the onion in the port and when cooked and the port reduced, add the truffles in their juice and the cream. • Allow to reduce by half and add the mushrooms and boletus. Bring to the boil quickly.

glossary of terms

Bain Marie

Method of cooking which heats the food without placing it directly on the heat, but rather in a bowl with water which is placed into the heat. This allows the temperature to be controlled and prevents overheating.

Bind

To add egg yolks or butter to a previously prepared sauce, beating to achieve a fine, well-mixed sauce, or adding a small amount of flour so that it thickens.

Boil

To place food in boiling water for a specific period so that it softens and becomes edible.

Boiling a lobster

Lobsters have to be cooked alive. Place the lobster in the boiling water, folding the tail downwards and tying it with two or three turns of twine, also tying up the claws and the antennae. Submerge completely in fiercely boiling water. Wait for the water to come to the boil again and leave to cook for 25 minutes.

Flambé

To sprinkle an ingredient or a dish with alcohol and set light to it.

Julienne

Very fine strips, normally of vegetables.

Marinate

To preserve certain foodstuffs raw, particularly fish, by leaving in a marinade of wine, vinegar, herbs, spices, etc, so that it softens and takes on flavour.

The marinade for tongue

(100 gr. nitrate salt, 300 gr. sea salt, 8 peeled garlic cloves, 6 peppercorns). Mix the sea salt with the garlic cloves and the peppercorns, and tip a third onto tin foil. Place the tongue on top and cover with the rest of the salt. Close the foil, twisting the edges and place in a deep dish, leaving it for 6 days in the fridge and removing the excess liquid every day.

Poach

Boil any ingredient on a low or medium heat until completely cooked.

Sauté

Lightly fry so that the ingredients turn golden before adding the stock or sauce in which they will be cooked. Can be in oil or butter.

Season

Add salt, pepper and/or spices to give taste.

Set

To solidify a liquid through heat through the addition of gelatine in the case of tongue; or adding a special rennet in the case of milk, or thickening it with flour and allowing it to cool.

Soak

Leave an ingredient in liquid to soften it.

Spread

Cover a preparation with sauce, cream etc.

Stew

To cook meat or fish, sauteing it first with a good quantity of onion, then bringing to the boil with the addition of a little stock.

Thicken

Give a liquid or mixture a denser consistency.

Truss

Tie up with twine or string the limbs of a fowl or pieces of fish or meat so that they maintain a particular shape during cooking.

subject index

115 tripe and other delicacies

121 sauces and pastry

127 glossary of terms

alphabetical index

Publication: Palacios y Museos
          Ana Cela
          Cristina Pineda
Text: Esperanza Luca de Tena
Translation: Laura Suffield
Photographs : © Cristina Rivarola
Design: Roser Domingo
          Cuca Roses
Collection design: Atela diseño gráfico
Layout: Myriam López Consalvi
Film-maker: Lucam
Printer: Gráficas Varona, S.A.
© Palacios y Museos, 2011
I.S.B.N.: 978-84-8003-920-8
Legal Deposit: S. 393-2011